# Jamal khashoggi: The Saudi Mystery

## By Dr Nasser Afify

# Table of Contents

# Chapter One: Introduction

Jamal Khashoggi, one of Saudi Arabia's most prominent journalists, hasn't been seen or heard from since he walked into the Saudi consulate in Istanbul on Oct. 2, 2018. He has been living in self-imposed exile in Virginia after leaving Saudi Arabia last year. Turkish officials have said he was killed inside the consulate, a claim the Saudi government has vehemently denied.

Khashoggi, 59, has been a leading critic of Saudi Arabia's current leadership, sharing his views via platforms including opinion columns in the Washington Post that began a year ago and were translated into Arabic. His journalism career has included stints in Afghanistan, where he met and followed the rise of al-Qaeda chief Osama bin Laden in the 1980s. He was deputy editor-in-chief of the Saudi newspaper Arab News at the time of the Sept. 11, 2001, attacks on the U.S., which made him a valuable source for foreign journalists seeking to understand what drove some Muslims into such actions. In the 2000s, he was twice fired from his post as editor-in-chief of the Saudi Al-Watan daily newspaper, which under his leadership ran stories, editorials and cartoons critical of extremists and the way in which the country enforced its religious values. (Saudi newspapers are privately owned but government-guided, and the government approves and can fire top leadership).

He told friends and reporters that the space for freedom of speech under Crown Prince Mohammed bin Salman was shrinking and he feared for his safety. In an appearance on Al Jazeera TV's "Upfront" that aired in March, he said he'd left the kingdom "because I don't want to be arrested." On the worsening environment for journalists since Prince Mohammed took over, he said, "I got fired from my job twice because I was pushing for reform in Saudi Arabia. It wasn't that easy but people were not being put in jails. There was a breathing space."

Khashoggi doesn't see himself as a dissident but as a critic worried about the direction his country is going under its 33-year-old crown prince. In his first Washington Post column on Sept. 18, 2017, he wrote about his decision to leave Saudi Arabia: "I have left my home, my family and my job, and I am raising my voice. To do otherwise would betray those who languish in prison. I can speak when so many cannot. I want you to know that Saudi Arabia has not always been as it is now. We Saudis deserve better." In February, Khashoggi wrote that Prince Mohammed maybe "should learn from the British royal house that has earned true stature, respect and success by trying a little humility himself. If MBS can listen to his critics and acknowledge that they, too, love their country, he can actually enhance his power." In the last column before his disappearance, he urged Prince Mohammed to end the war he started on Yemen more than three and a half years ago: "The longer this cruel war lasts in Yemen, the more permanent the damage will be. The people of Yemen will be busy fighting poverty, cholera and water scarcity and rebuilding their country. The crown prince must bring an end to the violence and restore the dignity of the birthplace of Islam."

Saudi authorities have refrained from saying anything critical about Khashoggi since his disappearance. Prince Mohammed said in a Bloomberg interview in Riyadh last week that Khashoggi is "a Saudi citizen and we are very keen to know what happened to him." His brother, Prince Khalid bin Salman, who's the kingdom's ambassador to Washington, called Khashoggi a "friend" and praised him for dedicating "a great portion of his life to serve his country."

In Turkey, they're known as the Kasikci family. Their most famous member until now was Adnan Khashoggi, the billionaire arms dealer whose biography is called "The Richest Man in the World," and who in the 1980s sold his yacht, the Nabila, to Donald

Trump. Adnan Khashoggi's father was Turkish, a doctor who married a Saudi woman and became court physician to King Abdulaziz, the founder of modern Saudi Arabia. That marked the family's rise to prominence in Saudi Arabia. However, they've kept their ties to Turkey. Another member of the family, Hasan Khashoggi, made the news in Turkey in 2017 when he survived a terrorist attack on the Reina nightclub in Istanbul, in which a gunman massacred 39 people.

# Chapter Two:

# An Interview with Jamal Khashoggi

The following is an excerpt from Jamestown Correspondent Mahan Abedin's interview with Jamal Khashoggi, A Saudi journalist and media advisor to the Saudi Ambassador to the UK, Prince Turki al-Faisal. He was previously editor-in-chief of the Saudi daily al-Watan. The interview was conducted July 7, 2004 at the Saudi embassy in London.

Mahan Abedin: Could you give a description of the terrorism threat that now confronts Saudi Arabia?

Jamal Khashoggi: Okay, I see it as a problem not a crisis, but nonetheless it should be treated as a crisis. It is not a threat or an insurgency that can topple the government. However, it is a problem that affects the three most important assets of Saudi Arabia, namely Islam, oil and stability. The blow to our stability has been acutely felt, given that Saudi Arabia was previously renowned as one of the safest and most stable countries in the world. We were proud of this fact and are anxious to regain this reputation. More broadly, I see this threat not as a permanent fixture in Saudi Arabia but rather as a passing phase. It is only a matter of time before we overwhelm the forces of terror.

MA: It is interesting that you characterize the threat in a way that does not seem to pose an existential threat to the Saudi Royal family. Can we conclude from your assessment that your government sees this problem as a purely security matter and therefore will largely depend on the deployment of security measures to tackle the problem, or do you concede that there are deeper socio-economic and cultural forces at play here?

JK: I am not saying that we are going to rely on purely security measures to tackle this threat. The problem is that there are two sides of fanaticism in Saudi Arabia. There are violent and non-violent fanatics. The former are composed of al-Qaeda people and their allies. The latter while sharing the agenda of the terrorists, ultimately eschew violence on the basis that it is self-defeating.

MA: What is your government's plan to deal with the terrorist crisis that engulfed the Kingdom in May last year?

JK: Exactly what they are doing right now. The Saudi government is employing security measures to destroy the terrorists. These include extensive intelligence gathering operations, interrogation of detainees and the identification and storming of safe houses. There have been a series of successes on these fronts. At the same time the government is tackling the forces and ideas that justify terrorism and radicalism. Here we are facing a more difficult problem as there is no real agreement in Saudi Arabia on the root causes of terrorism. Some people go to extremes and accuse all Islamic elements of promoting terrorism. I disagree with this assessment. Some go to the other extreme and limit the exponents of violence to a small collection of extremists. I disagree with this assessment also, as I think the real problem is somewhere between the two. I think we should leave no stone unturned in the search for the causes of terrorism in our country. This is not a foreign phenomenon, these terrorists have not come from outer space as some people in Saudi Arabia like to suggest. Clearly there are foreign influences on the terrorists, but this does not divest us from our responsibilities.

[...]

MA: At the same time some official people in Saudi Arabia have made statements and proposals that seem to reflect the gravity of the crisis. For instance does Prince Nayef's recent announcement that the government may be willing to allow westerners to carry fire arms to protect themselves from potential terrorist attacks, indicate a division in the establishment as to the extent and gravity of the crisis?

JK: Carrying firearms in Saudi Arabia is allowed providing you have the appropriate license. This is our way of saying to our friends that we are considering all options to ensure your security. There are a small number of foreigners who have asked to be armed and they have been granted permission to carry firearms. However we do not envisage the widespread arming of the expatriate population.

[…]

MA: Okay, let us focus on the specifics of the terrorist threat. Why does your government insist that the slaying of Abdul Aziz Muqrin in June constituted a severe blow to al-Qaeda and the wider terrorist movement?

JK: It is a serious blow because he was a very significant leader. According to information gathered by our security Muqrin was a pivotal figure in the development of these terrorist networks. He was also an influential figure in the overall hierarchy of the terrorist structures. Muqrin worked tirelessly on behalf of al-Qaeda.

[…]

MA: What can you tell us about [Muqrin's replacement, al-Oufi]?

JK: He was just a junior guard in a prison in Medina. He was merely a low ranking officer.

MA: Are you saying that all the news stories we have heard regarding his security background and connections are over-stated?

JK: They are well over-stated. Al-Qaeda does not have prominent people in its ranks. Their most prominent member is a former college tutor.

MA: Are you referring to al-Rashoud?

JK: Yes, Sheikh al-Rashoud.

MA: He was killed recently in a shoot out, right?

JK: No, he was not killed.

[…]

MA: How many people have you detained over the past 15 months?

JK: It is between 600-1000.

MA: How are they being treated?

JK: According to my information they are being treated in a humane way. They have access to their families and they are undergoing sessions with Islamic scholars in order to appreciate the errors inherent in their bloody interpretation of Islam.

[…]

MA: What kind of help [are you getting help from other countries]?

JK: Mainly intelligence.

MA: You are receiving intelligence from foreign countries on your own country?

JK: Look, this fight is a global fight. Al-Qaeda works both within and outside Saudi Arabia. Their logistical and communications networks transcend borders and continents.

MA: So you don't make a distinction between al-Qaeda in Saudi Arabia and al-Qaeda as the global terrorist phenomenon?

JK: Absolutely not. They are all the same people. We have concrete evidence that even on the media front the terrorists in Saudi Arabia receive extensive help from those outside the country. I am referring here to the design of websites, newsletters and the production of articles. This is an international phenomenon and our counter-terrorism strategy takes this into account.

MA: Is it true that the FBI have access to the files of the 600-1000 detainees you alluded to earlier?

JK: I don't know. However if this is needed and both we and the Americans are going to benefit from it, I don't see a problem with this. It is no secret that we work closely with the Americans, British and the French. In fact we are working with anyone who can help us defeat this horrible phenomenon.

MA: But part of the problem you face is that your counter-terrorism strategy must address the grievances of your people. One of these grievances is that your government has an exceptionally close relationship with the Americans. Therefore extensive security cooperation of this kind may have undesirable long-term consequences.

JK: Not at all. The Americans are not a grievance in Saudi Arabia. The grievances revolve around poverty, unemployment and access to resources.

MA: You are denying that the widely held perception in the Middle East that the U.S. is unduly biased towards Israel is not a grievance in Saudi Arabia?

JK: It is not an issue. We care about the Palestinians but we are reasonable people. We have had relations with the Americans for decades, just like many other Muslim countries. Therefore Saudi Arabia is by no means unique in this sense. Even the terrorists drive American cars!

MA: I have been told by reliable sources that up to 12,000 people have been detained and interrogated at the behest of the Americans. Is there any credence to these allegations?

JK: I don't know. But I would say that it is in Saudi Arabia's interest to leave no stone unturned in this fight against terrorism.

[…]

MA: Okay, what kind of numbers are we talking about overall [in terms of professional terrorists in Saudi Arabia]?

JK: The numbers are put below 500.

MA: And these are professional al-Qaeda people who are exclusively dedicated to fighting the Saudi regime?

JK: Yes.

[…]

MA: I have been told by a reliable source that there are several hundred detainees in al-Ruwais prison in Jeddah. The detainees are apparently former Mujahideen fighters…and they are not known to have promoted violence against the Saudi regime. Therefore should not the amnesty apply to these people as well?

JK: This is not true. I can say with certainty, because I covered the Afghan conflict as a journalist, that 99% of the Saudis who fought in that conflict have had no problems with our government. They returned to Saudi Arabia and were on the whole re-integrated into society. However the self-proclaimed Saudi Mujahideen who went to Afghanistan after 1996, were arrested not because they went to

Afghanistan, but because they joined al-Qaeda. They gave their allegiance to an organization and a man whose aim is to overthrow the Saudi state. We should distinguish between Arab Mujahideen who went to Afghanistan from the mid 1980s to 1992, and those who made their way to Afghanistan after this date.

[…]

MA: Okay, let us focus on peaceful political reform in Arabia. Why can't you extend the amnesty we discussed earlier to peaceful reformers in the Kingdom?

JK: There is no widespread detention of reformers in Saudi Arabia. The detained reformers you are referring to are basically three individuals. There is Dr. Abdullah al-Hamed, the poet Ali al-Dumaini, and the last person I can't remember his name.

MA: Matrouk al-Falleh?

JK: Yes, that is right.

MA: There is of course Said bin Zubair.

JK: No, Said bin Zubair is not a reformer, he is al-Qaeda material.

MA: This is interesting insofar as it hints at interconnections between the peaceful and the violent reformers.

JK: There is no connection between them whatsoever. Please don't confuse the two.

[…]

MA: [Moving on to Iran and Iraq. Do you think] Iran would hand over senior detained al-Qaeda people to the U.S. in return for the dismantling of the Mojahedin-e-Khalq's organization in Iraq?

JK: I am really surprised that the Americans have not dismantled the Mojahedin-e-Khalq infrastructure in Iraq. This is really strange and the Americans need to explain their position. It is not right for any country to host its neighbor's enemies. And we all know that the Mojahedin-e-Khalq is a particularly extreme terrorist organization and it is not right for Iraq to be hosting them. I don't blame the Iranians for feeling frustrated on this issue.

[…]

MA: I have heard that the Iranian government has extradited numerous al-Qaeda people to Saudi Arabia in the past 30 months.

JK: Yes, they have.

[…]

MA: How are the Israelis involved in Iraq?

JK: The Americans are copying Israeli counter-insurgency tactics. Moreover there are reports that Israelis are on the ground in

Iraq advising the American authorities. This is the most stupid thing that the Americans could have done. I will give you another example. For some time now Saudi Arabia has applied to join the WTO, but the Americans are putting pressure on us to end our boycott of Israel. Our boycott of Israel is driven by politics, not economics. We boycott Israel because they happen to be occupying Palestinian lands. As long as America does not reverse its Pro-Israel bias, it will continue to experience problems in the Middle East. The only problems we have with America revolve around Israel.

[…]

MA: Do you think the invasion of Iraq has heightened the terrorist threat?

JK: Yes, it has. It has not helped the Americans as they have made one mistake after another. They just love making mistakes.

# Chapter Three:

## Ending Yemen's cruel war

He said that Saudi Arabia must face the damage from the past three-plus years of war in Yemen. The conflict has soured the kingdom's relations with the international community, affected regional security dynamics and harmed its reputation in the Islamic world. Saudi Arabia is in a unique position to simultaneously keep Iran out of Yemen and end the war on favorable terms if it change its role from warmaker to peacemaker. Saudi Arabia could use its clout and leverage within Western circles and empower international institutions and mechanisms to resolve the conflict. However, the window for achieving a resolution to the conflict is rapidly closing.

The-U.N. sponsored Geneva peace talks that were scheduled to open last Thursday have practically collapsed, in part because Houthis rebels who control the capitol (and most of western Yemen) were afraid their return would be halted due to Saudi Arabia's control of Yemen's airspace. The Saudis could provide their enemy and the U.N. officials with travel support — or perhaps they could even offer them a Saudi plane. Even better, Saudi Arabia could announce a cease-fire and offer peace talks in the Saudi Arabian city of Taif, where previous peace talks with Yemenis have taken place.

Saudi Arabia's actions in Yemen were driven by national security concerns due to Iranian involvement in the country. However, Saudi Arabia's war efforts have not provided an extra layer of security but have rather increased the likelihood of domestic casualties and damage. Saudi defense systems rely on the U.S.-made Patriot missile system. Saudi Arabia has been successful in preventing Houthi missiles from causing substantial damage. Yet, the inability of Saudi authorities in preventing Houthi missiles from being fired in the first place serves as an embarrassing reminder that the kingdom's leadership is unable to restrain their Iranian-backed opponent.

Each missile fired by Houthi forces poses both a political and financial burden on the kingdom. The cost of an Iranian missile supplied to the Houthis is uncertain, but one can speculate that each missile does not compare to the cost of a $3 million Patriot missile.

Unexpected costs associated with the conflict in Yemen means Saudi Arabia has increasingly been borrowing funds in international markets without clearly saying what the funds are for. The kingdom has reportedly raised $11 billion in a loan from international banks.

Furthermore, the political costs associated with the loss of innocent life cannot be tabulated. Lapses in Saudi Intel led to the deployment of a bomb to target a bus suspected of carrying Houthi forces. Instead, the missile struck a school bus carrying children. The kingdom cannot afford to have an open war zone at its southern border, the confidence of international markets and the moral high ground.

Mistakes and risks associated with long-term conflict diminish Saudi standing internationally and increase the chances of a confrontation with traditional allies. Defense Secretary Jim Mattis recently stated, "We support our partner Saudi Arabia's right to self-defense." The Saudi media ran Mattis's statement and quoted him with great enthusiasm but selectively omitted the portion that stated American support was "not unconditional" and that he urged Saudi authorities to "do everything humanly possible to avoid any innocent loss of life."

Mattis's remarks should serve as a reality check to Saudi Crown Prince Mohammed bin Salman. Saudi Arabia is defined and represented by its Islamic stature. We should not need to be reminded of the value of human life. Muslims around the world deserve to see birthplace of Islam represent the ethics of Islam.

Saudi Arabia does not deserve to be compared to Syria, whose leader seemingly did not hesitate to use chemical weapons against his people. But further continuation of the war in Yemen will validate voices saying that Saudi Arabia is doing in Yemen what Syrian President Bashar al-Assad, the Russians and Iranians are doing in Syria. Even the south of Yemen that has been "liberated," protesters are currently staging a civil disobedience campaign, chanting slogans against the Saudi-led coalition, which is seen as the actual power on the ground, rather than Yemen's exiled government.

Peace talks will provide Saudi Arabia with a golden opportunity. Riyadh will almost certainly find international support if it enters into a cease-fire as negotiations take place. It must utilize its global clout and incorporate international institutions and allies to financially pressure Tehran to stand down in Yemen. The Saudi Arabian crown prince must also accept that the Houthis, the Islah (Sunni Islamists) and the southern separatists should play a future role in the governance of Yemen. Obviously, Riyadh will not get all of what it wants and would leave Yemenis to sort out their differences with their fellow Houthis in a National Congress — instead of on bloody battlefields.

The longer this cruel war lasts in Yemen, the more permanent the damage will be. The people of Yemen will be busy fighting poverty, cholera and water scarcity and rebuilding their country. The crown prince must bring an end to the violence and restore the dignity of the birthplace of Islam.

# Chapter Four:

## Fighting Canada

He said that Saudi Arabia seems to have mistaken Canada, a member of the Group of Seven and NATO, and a distinguished ally of many European nations, for the small Middle Eastern nation of Qatar, which Riyadh blockaded last June.

Arrest of Samar Badawi, the sister of imprisoned blogger Raif Badawi, led Canada's Foreign Ministry to issue a statement in Arabic on its Twitter account that urged "the Saudi authorities to immediately release" her, along with fellow activist Nassima al-Sadah. It was this tweet that sparked the ire of Saudi authorities and propelled them into taking action. Saudi Arabia responded by recalling its ambassador in Ottawa, freezing trade relations, withdrawing Saudi students from Canadian schools and even canceling flights between Saudi Arabia and Toronto.

When Canada's embassy in Riyadh tweeted its government's statement in Arabic, Saudi officials saw it as a challenge to national sovereignty on domestic social media, which has increasingly become the battleground to control national public opinion and promote hyper-nationalism. Saudi Arabia's Crown Prince Mohammed bin Salman, known by his initials, MBS, is signaling that any open opposition to Saudi domestic policies, even ones as egregious as the punitive arrests of reform-seeking Saudi women, is intolerable. The West should not ignore human rights abuses in the Arab world, but its indifference to the cruelty of Arab regimes in Syria and Egypt — where hundreds of thousands have been killed or imprisoned — has encouraged the spread of authoritarian rule in countries that once had a restrained appetite for pursuing such policies.

Presently, Saudi citizens no longer understand the rationale behind the relentless wave of arrests. These arbitrary arrests are forcing many into silence, and a few others have even quietly left the country. To Riyadh, "vigorously defending Saudi Arabia's sovereignty" means "using punitive measures against transnational civil society groups and the countries that support them," tweeted Kristin Diwan, a senior resident scholar at the Arab Gulf States Institute in Washington.

Of course, there is a better way for the kingdom to avoid Western criticism: Simply free human rights activists, and stop the unnecessary arrests that have diminished the Saudi image. Doing so will salvage what is left of the reputation that the crown prince worked so hard to build during his multiweek tour of Europe and the United States earlier this year.

Saudi Arabia simply cannot afford to alienate any other sections of the global community in the midst of its unpopular military engagement in Yemen, its indirect confrontation with Iran. Most importantly, Saudi Arabia's economic transformation requires more friends than enemies. For MBS to achieve the economic and transformative vision that he espoused on his foreign tour, he needs to use ways and means that investors are accustomed to. If business executives fear a backlash over any possible criticism regarding their investment, the new vision of Saudi Arabia would be in serious jeopardy.

Instead of lashing out at Canada, shouldn't we ask why peace-loving Canada has turned against us? We, Saudi citizens, need to see the bigger picture. Canada raised the flag against human rights abuses in Saudi Arabia. Surely, we cannot arbitrarily arrest female activists and expect the world to turn a blind eye.

Criticism of the Middle East should not be directed only at Saudi Arabia. Human rights abuses are happening throughout the Arab world. For example, Egypt has jailed 60,000 opposition members and is deserving of criticism as well. The slaughter of innocent civilians in Syria and Yemen should also be highlighted, not because criticism is unfair to Saudi Arabia, but because failing to criticize creates an atmosphere that empowers authoritarian rulers to deny civil rights to their own people.

Many Arabs who seek freedom, equality and democracy feel defeated. They have been portrayed as traitors by pro-government media and abandoned by the international community. Canada's stand, therefore, restores their hope that someone out there does indeed still care.

# Chapter Five:

## Saudi Arabia's women can finally drive

He said that he streets of Saudi Arabia were alive with the sounds of women revving car engines and driving. For the first time, they were allowed to operate motor vehicles without fear of arrest and detention. Under the driving ban, if a woman was arrested, she was held until a male guardian came and picked her up — but only after he signed a pledge that she would not drive again.

For decades, Saudi society was divided over the issue of women driving between the so-called liberals and the religious bloc. The latter presented the issue as a matter of "Halal and Haram" through the sharia (Islamic law), making it difficult to even debate — even though many other Muslim countries have allowed women to drive cars. Fatwas of prohibition were issued by senior official scholars in Saudi Arabia.

The media had its hands tied. The Saudi government was not keen to have a public debate about women driving. It guided the newspapers toward shutting down the conversation anytime it began to gain traction in society. It also played the neutrality card between liberals and the more religious Saudis. Moreover, some senior princes, like late Crown Prince Nayef, opposed letting women drive.

He had been a powerful figure for decades and ran the Interior Ministry, holding sway over what happened in the kingdom.

His objection, like that of so many, wasn't really on religious grounds as much as it was based on male chauvinism. Many Saudi clerics believe that letting women drive means they will be free to leave the house whenever they like — something that will have a liberalizing and therefore unwanted effect on society. Sheikh Saleh al-Fawzan, a member of the Council of Senior Scholars, said as much in a televised interview. He certainly won't be saying that now, not after the government has gone ahead with lifting the ban.

Prince Sultan, a former crown prince and defense minister, was more diplomatic. He said it was not the government that had a problem with letting women drive, but rather, the people. Saudi officials found in his statements an opportunity to evade the question whenever the Western media raised the issue. The tenor of his opposition, though, actually encouraged the pro-driving movement now enjoying the taste of victory. The movement was led by an emerging generation of Saudi women such as Manal al-Sharif (now living in Australia) and Loujain al-Hathloul (recently detained by Saudi authorities) who got behind the wheel in Saudi

Arabia, videotaped it and posted the footage to social media to emphasize the need for change.

The Saudi media had the responsibility to cover the debate, even though we knew the government did not want it publicized. Many officials wanted to solve this dilemma, due in part to economic pressures, as well as the increased numbers of women working thanks to the education they were getting for the first time. When females were finally allowed to enroll in Saudi universities, they eventually exceeded the number of males, yet this was not reflected in the labor market.

As editor of the newspaper Al-Watan in 2007, I bypassed the ban on public debate over the issue by publishing a series of clever articles by the brilliant writer Abdullah al-Fawzan. He imagined a girl riding a camel to her university and the ensuing predicament. The school doesn't know where to park the camel. The policeman cannot figure out how to deal with the camel. The girl, meanwhile, rides to school on a road alongside car drivers who don't know what to make of the camel because the law does not prohibit it. If she was driving a car, the policeman's task was made easier; any official had instructions to take the girl to the police station and contact her legal guardian.

At the time it was published, it was a controversial article. We received letters in support of the piece, but those who opposed women driving were organized and more persistent. A week later, we ran the same article but now the girl was driving a bicycle. Then we ran another story in which she was riding a donkey. That way, we kept the issue alive while waiting for the government to make a change.

On television, three years ago, I debated a hard-line cleric who based his arguments against women driving on religion. He talked about the "freedom of women" and the destruction of society. Beyond banning women from driving, he offered other repressive ideas for suppressing women's participation in society. We need to remember that women in Saudi Arabia did not get their right to education until the 1960s, and only after a similar fight.

Eventually, I had to give up my part in keeping the national conversation alive. My decision was brought to the attention of the most famous female TV personality in Saudi Arabia, Badriya Al Bishr(the Saudi Oprah Winfrey), who asked me on air why I took this stance.

"The different parties presented their argument more than once," I told her, "and the government needs to step up and make the decision." I said that the government should be courageous and bring an otherwise sterile debate to an end. I wasn't optimistic that a quick decision was in the offing. I had become tired of going around in circles. The government always had multiple economic, social and political reasons to allow women to drive. It simply lacked the courage to move ahead.

Crown Prince Mohammed bin Salman deserves consider credit for bringing the matter to a close the right way. While previous leaders were reluctant to take up the issue, he faced it head-on and did the right thing for Saudi Arabia. At the same time, I hope he will not forget the brave actions of each and every Saudi who individually worked hard for freedom and modernization. He should order the release of Hathloul, Aziza al-Yousef, Eman al-Nafjan and the other brave women who campaigned for women's right to drive. They should be allowed to finally witness the results of their tears and toil.

# Chapter Six:

## Saudi Arabia's reformers

He said that it is appalling to see 60- and 70-year-old icons of reform being branded as "traitors" on the front pages of Saudi newspapers.

Women and men who championed many of the same social freedoms —including women driving— that Crown Prince Mohammed bin Salman is now advancing were arrested in Saudi Arabia last week. The crackdown has shocked even the government's most stalwart defenders.

The arrests illuminate the predicament confronting all Saudis. We are being asked to abandon any hope of political freedom, and to keep quiet about arrests and travel bans that impact not only the critics but also their families. We are expected to vigorously applaud social reforms and heap praise on the crown prince while avoiding any reference to the pioneering Saudis who dared to address these issues decades ago.

Last week's arrests were simply about controlling the narrative. The message is clear to all: Activism of any sort has to be within the government, and no independent voice or counter-opinion will be allowed. Everyone must stick to the party line.

Is there no other way for us? Must we choose between movie theaters and our rights as citizens to speak out, whether in support of or critical of our government's actions? Do we only voice glowing references to our leader's decisions, his vision of our future, in exchange for the right to live and travel freely — for ourselves and our wives, husbands and children too? I have been told that I need to accept, with gratitude, the social reforms that I have long called for while keeping silent on other matters — ranging from the Yemen quagmire, hastily executed economic reforms, the blockade of Qatar, discussions about an alliance with Israel to counter Iran, and last year's imprisonment of dozens of Saudi intellectuals and clerics.

This is the choice I've woken up to each morning ever since last June, when I left Saudi Arabia for the last time after being silenced by the government for six months.

I wonder if, like me, Lujain Al-Hathloul, one of the most prominent Saudi women activists who were arrested last week, has struggled with such dilemmas. Or if her lawyer, Ibrahim Modeimigh, deals with these inner conflicts, too. State Security accused them and others of being involved in activities that "encroach on religious and national constants; the group had suspicious contact with external parties supporting their activities and recruiting people working in sensitive government positions."

In short, though she complied with the government's order to be silent about her decades of work in support of women driving, and even allowed the crown price alone to take credit for lifting the driving ban, she and her associates are being punished for speaking with the foreign media tasked with covering next month's lifting of the ban and other social changes in Saudi Arabia.

There is nothing remarkable about having media and foreign embassy contacts. When I lived in Saudi Arabia as a journalist, this was a regular occurrence. It's happening even more often given the pace of government-promoted reforms. Yet now, unlike two or three years ago, any foreign contact that deviates from the approved script is treasonous. Yes, treasonous –that is the word that was used to publicly defame those arrested.

I have never witnessed such a draconian response to anything as innocuous as simply speaking with foreign journalists and officials. It does not align with the good impressions of openness and reforms that the crown prince successfully reinforced during his recent visit to Europe and the United States. It undercuts his interviews with journalists and off-the-record editorial board meetings with major newspapers — including The Washington Post, where he spent about two hours talking to editors about his reform policies. Religious fanaticism that had tarnished Saudi Arabia's image for decades has given way to a new and perhaps more pernicious fanaticism, a cult of blind loyalty to our leader.

This is a Faustian bargain that I will not make. I suspect Lujain and her associates may have felt the same way.

I expect that I will still wake up every morning and ponder the choice I have made to speak my mind about what is happening in Saudi Arabia. It is a pattern that I have grown accustomed to. Despite the anguish it causes me, it reminds me of how much I miss my country and my home. But now, after these fresh arrests and the public humiliation of these individuals, my doubts are greatly diminished. The social reforms that are so important to Saudi Arabia cannot come at the expense of the public space once available to us for discussion and debate. Repression and intimidation are not — and never should be– the acceptable companions of reform.

# Chapter Seven:

## What Saudi Arabia can learn from 'Black Panther'?

He said that this Wednesday, Disney's blockbuster "Black Panther" will be shown in theaters in Saudi Arabia, officially ending a decades-long ban on movie theaters in the country. This may seem odd to Americans who have grown up with cinema and popcorn, but to many Saudis it's a huge step toward normalization. For too long, hard-line religious figures have preached that cinema would bring about the collapse of all moral values. When the Saudi Crown Prince Mohammed bin Salman decided to end the ban, he also effectively stopped the preachers from repeating such foolishness. By taking the lead to remove the ban, he proved that the government has the final say when it comes to deciding what's permissible or not, and that some things should be left up to the personal choice of citizens, not the clergy.

Because there haven't been cinemas in Saudi Arabia for more than 30 years, Saudi newspapers don't have movie reviews. I can only imagine what the plot and symbols of the film will prompt critics to write. Will they dare to tease out references to local politics?

In "Black Panther," T'Challa (Chadwick Boseman), the young king of Wakanda, grapples with whether to hide his wealthy and prosperous country from the outside world, or to engage with it — a question that preoccupies Saudis these days, especially given the turbulence and civil wars surrounding them in the Middle East.

Saudi Arabia does have plenty of money and oil, even if it doesn't have Wakanda's "vibranium" (a super-substance that powers the country's technology). What Saudis do lack, however, is the amazing scientific development that Wakanda enjoys. The crown prince is hoping to change that. In his recent U.S. tour, he made a point of meeting the leaders of the technology companies who are at the forefront of the global information revolution.

Many other countries in the region also have money and oil, but they haven't done much good with it — at least not enough to stop the Middle East's disastrous wars. Saudi Arabia at least has something else: stability, a scarce commodity in the region. (And if the crown prince has his way, the kingdom will also soon benefit from economic reform, which is designed to provide jobs for millions of young Saudis.) But Riyadh still lacks a proper recipe for restoring peace to the Middle East and creating a new prosperous and peaceful world.

Indeed, Saudi Arabia's vibranium should be its stability, financial strength and strong foreign relations. And if the kingdom wants to go a step further, moving to encourage democracy and popular participation in the Middle East would be the most effective means of ensuring regional stability well as protecting itself from neighboring threats.

It might seem odd to call on a country that lacks democracy, such as Saudi Arabia, to use it to restore peace around it. The difference is that Saudis need democracy for better governance, while Syrians and Yemenis need it to stop killing one another. None of these wars will be won militarily. But Saudi Arabia can certainly do more to play a constructive role to bring peace to those countries. Riyadh can encourage the formations of pluralistic governments in both countries and put pressure on the factions there to agree to negotiations.

At the end of the film, the young king of Wakanda chooses to use his country's power to engage with the world for the greater good. Will Crown Prince Mohammed bin Salman, who likely will soon become king of his country, use his power to bring peace to the world around him?

# Chapter Eight:

## Blaming 1979 for Saudi Arabia's problems

He said that in an interview with the news program "60 Minutes," Crown Prince Mohammed Bin Salman said of Saudi Arabia before 1979, "We were living a very normal life like the rest of the Gulf countries. Women were driving cars, there were movie theaters in Saudi Arabia, and women worked everywhere. We were normal people developing like any other country in the world until the events of 1979."

I was a teenager in the 1970s and grew up in Medina, Saudi Arabia. My memories of those years before the twin disasters of 1979 — the siege of the Grand Mosque of Mecca and the Iranian Revolution — are quite different from the narrative that the 32-year old crown prince (known as MBS for short) advances to Western audiences. Women weren't driving cars. I didn't see a woman drive until I visited my sister and brother-in-law in Tempe, Ariz., in 1976. The movie theaters we had were makeshift, like American drive-ins except much more informal. The movie was beamed on a big wall. You would pay 5 or 10 riyals (then approximately $1.50-$2) to the organizer, who would then give a warning when the religious police approached. To avoid being arrested, a friend of mine broke his leg jumping off a wall. In the 1970s, the only places on the Arabian Peninsula where women were working outside the home or school were Kuwait and Bahrain.

The first rule that affected Saudi women's rights was not the result of a campaign by Wahhabi religious authorities or a fatwa. Many Saudis remember the sad story of a 19-year-old Saudi princess who tried to flee the country with her lover. They were both executed in 1977; the episode was the subject of a 1980 British documentary drama "Death of a Princess." The reaction of the government to the princess's elopement was swift: The segregation of women became more severe, and no woman could travel without the consent of a male relative.

In 1980, the minister of industry and electricity, Ghazi al-Gosaibi, sent a handwritten letter to King Khalid warning against restrictive measures on women's images appearing in print and on TV media. He asked the king to revise these policies "so we would not be made an example of rigidity and stagnation in front of the whole world." He was ignored.

MBS would like to advance a new narrative for my country's recent history, one that absolves the government of any complicity in the adoption of strict Wahhabi doctrine. That simply isn't the case. And while MBS is right to free Saudi Arabia from ultra-conservative religious forces, he is wrong to advance a new radicalism that, while seemingly more liberal and appealing to the West, is just as intolerant of dissent.

In the 1950s and 1960s, Saudi Arabia welcomed Egyptians who fled Egypt fearing that the president, Gamal Abdel Nasser, would imprison them for their beliefs. Many were part of the Muslim Brotherhood. They brought with them new approaches to Islamic thought and law that were welcomed by many of us, including our leaders.

King Faisal, who was assassinated in 1975, set up the first public schools for girls in the 1960s, a move staunchly opposed by the religious establishment. In his struggle to bring the country into the 21st century, he thought the Muslim Brotherhood could be a counterweight to the Wahhabi clerics.

King Faisal entrusted the highly respected Sheikh Manaa al-Qattan to modernize the Saudi judiciary. Reforms not otherwise possible began due to the scholarship of members of the Muslim Brotherhood, including labor laws, teaching of English and chemistry, and the partial creation of a legal code. Now the Saudi media, at the encouragement of the government, vilifies al-Qattan, saying he was a member of the Muslim Brotherhood. Why is that suddenly so objectionable?

In Saudi Arabia at the moment, people simply don't dare to speak. The country has seen the blacklisting of those who dare raise their voices, the imprisonment of moderately critical intellectuals and religious figures, and the alleged anti-corruption crackdown on royals and other business leaders. Liberals whose work was once censored or banned by Wahhabi hard-liners have turned the tables: They now ban what they see as hard-line, such as the censorship of various books at the Riyadh International Book Fair last month. One may applaud such an about-face. But shouldn't we aspire to allow the marketplace of ideas to be open?

I agree with MBS that the nation should return to its pre-1979 climate, when the government restricted hard-line Wahhabi traditions. Women today should have the same rights as men. And all citizens should have the right to speak their minds without fear of imprisonment. But replacing old tactics of intolerance with new ways of repression is not the answer.

# Chapter Nine:

# Queen Elizabeth II

Saudi Arabia's Crown Prince Mohammed bin Salman, known as MBS, likes to proclaim his reforms using a bit of "shock therapy." He vowed to "divorce" Islamic radicals, declaring theatrically, "We will destroy them!" His war on corruption, marked by imprisoning members of the royal family in Riyadh's Ritz-Carlton, was launched via social media. It became a national nail-biter for Saudi citizens, and even more so for thousands of the royal Saud family members and non-royal titans of business.

Last month's arrest of 11 more royals added a new dimension to the unfolding drama: the possible restructuring of the Saudi royal family.

There is talk that MBS might remove royal designations for those without a direct connection to King Abdul Aziz, like Saud al-Kabir's branch of the royal family. If so, it would represent the first major and unprecedented restructuring of the royal family. "Al-Kabir" means "the Grand" or "the Mighty," but members of the clan are, in fact, junior relatives descending from a royal cousin, Saud al-Kabir, head of a branch of the family known as the "araif" — a Bedouin word for camels lost in a raid, then recaptured. These camels of dubious loyalty joined forces with the Sauds' deadly rivals, the Rasheeds, in the 19th century, to bring down the second Saudi state — a Shakespearean saga of treachery, blood and betrayal, whose elements of family strife do not appear in the Saudi school curriculum.

MBS's goal is clear: He wants to tamp down a suffocating and ever-expanding tangle of royals and subordinates and prevent strife. Since Abdul Aziz's death in 1953, Saudi Arabia has inherited dynastic structures that allowed independent power centers to develop and multiply.

That led to an endless appetite for wealth, greed encouraged by unchecked power. The royals monopolized land and businesses all over the kingdom. On top of all that, they received guaranteed monthly stipends and generous grants.

Indeed, the wealth of the royals has quietly irked Saudi citizens. One of the most pervasive myths about the kingdom is that all Saudis are fabulously wealthy. Most of them are not. According to 2016 World Bank data, per capita income in Saudi Arabia is lower than in the United States, the United Kingdom and most Gulf neighbors. A few days before last month's arrests, King Salman ordered all royals to pay their water, electric and telephone bills. Given the lavish lifestyle of the Saud family, many owning more than one palatial home, the bills add up to a staggering sum.

So, when members of the Saud al-Kabir family allegedly protested the imposition of these routine domestic expenses, their arrests were widely praised. Though they are not direct descendants of the country's founder, King Abdul Aziz, they have been endowed with scores of government and private business interests. One of the gang who complained was rapidly fired from his post at the Saudi sport federation, and yet another might stand trial for treason.

For lessons in managing minor royals and family strife, the young crown prince might heed the example of Queen Elizabeth II, whom he will be visiting on his way to Washington next month. The House of Windsor ruthlessly rations its "HRH" titles to core relatives around the sovereign — the al-Kabirs and many others would have been off the royal radar (and the payroll) generations ago according to the rules of the world's most successful reigning family.

The Windsors also appreciate the virtues of age and experience. Figures such as the late Queen Mother, and now Queen Elizabeth II herself, rival the glamorous young William, Catherine, Harry and Meghan in the popularity stakes. So, while MBS is moving in the right direction if he is preparing to "downsize" the House of Saud, cutting out the "Game of Thrones"-like tangle of rivalrous royalties, he should not forget the value of such wise older heads as the experienced and diplomatic Prince Turki al-Faisal. Might his mature skills resolve the tragic standoff in Yemen.

The greatest lesson the House of Saud might learn from the House of Windsor is to listen to the people — "What touches all should be approved by all." Elizabeth II has enhanced her stature on several occasions by bowing her head to public criticism, notably after the death of Princess Diana in 1997. The Queen was judged the grander for showing humility — Elizabeth "al-Kabira" — and she is proud to preside over a society where thought and speech are free.

The same cannot be said for Saudi Arabia. The arrest of those 11 princes may seem like good news — for the first time in modern history, royals are being treated like ordinary citizens. But what about the several dozen intellectuals, religious scholars and journalists who, with far less international attention, have been awaiting trial in Saudi Arabia since last September, some of them in solitary confinement while the state tries in vain to find grounds to charge them? Unlike the arrested royals, they never protested in front of the governor's palace, did not raise their voices demanding to meet with the king and did not resist when the police tried to disperse them — they had never met or demonstrated. Their only form of protest was their ideas.

MBS's downsizing and relative humbling of the House of Saud is welcome news. But maybe he should learn from the British royal house that has earned true stature, respect and success by trying a little humility himself. If MBS can listen to his critics and acknowledge that they, too, love their country, he can actually enhance his power.

# Chapter Ten:

# Fighting Corruption in Saudi Arabia

He said that in the whirlwind of headlines about Saudi Crown Prince Mohammed bin Salman and his highly visible campaign against corruption, one might forget that barely a week earlier, he was courting titans of global industry, technology and finance at an investment conference that was also the launch of NEOM, a gleaming futuristic metropolis. As Dave Eggers writes in "A Hologram for the King", in which an American salesman travels to Saudi Arabia to visit a similarly promising marvel, "There were people in the world for whom the world and its people were subjects on which to cast spells."

The spell was broken when dozens of royals, along with current and former senior officials, were detained at the Ritz Carlton, accused of corruption. A few have been released after reportedly paying billions in what looks increasingly more like a shakedown than a legally-grounded pursuit of justice. More recently, there are rumors that the state will place some private companies under the custody of the government's Public Investment Fund, further entangling business and government, preventing the Saudi economy from realizing its full potential. Shares of Kingdom Holding, the principal holding of Prince Waleed bin Talal, declined more than 21 percent ($2.8 billion) after his arrest. Such strong-arm tactics deter foreign investors who wonder, "If the government goes after such prominent Saudi citizens, what might they do to us?"

As a Saudi journalist starting my career right after the oil boom of the 1970s, I witnessed the phenomenal growth and expansion of Saudi businesses and the pivotal role the leaders of these firms played in building the modern Saudi economy. They were inextricably connected with the Saudi government, which provided access to capital, and other forms of legitimate support that accelerated their growth. There were other consequences of this rapid development, including rampant corruption that touched every aspect of society, including members of Saudi Arabia's ruling family, the Al-Saud. Now, as the deeply flawed anti-corruption campaign targets royals and notable business leaders, what has been lost is an appreciation for this generation of business pioneers and, more critically, their role in growing and diversifying the economy to employ millions of Saudi youth.

The story of close cooperation between entrepreneurs and government officials is not unique to Saudi Arabia. The stunning fall of President Park Geun-hye last year exposed a similar system in South Korea. As the Korean War ended, her father and former President Park Chun-hee enticed businessmen and capitalists with cheap credit and exclusive privileges to rebuild the nation, and in return, shared in the company profits. This strategy led to the emergence of giant family-owned businesses (Chaebols), many of which have become household names such as Samsung and Hyundai. These businesses rebuilt South Korea and made it an industrial giant on the world stage.

South Korea handled corruption much differently. The presidential trial played out in public with a court delivering the verdict. The businesses involved were insulated from the ousting of President Park and her government. Their day-to-day financial operations and profitability were not impacted. Following the ousting of President Park, South Korea's top regulator even issued a statement stating Park's departure would not impact market stability.

The opposite is occurring in Saudi Arabia. One Arab businessman told me, "Saudi Arabia is at a crossroads. For Vision 2030 to succeed, transparency, justice, and equal opportunity — as called for by MbS — are prerequisites. The events to fight corruption over the past year, specifically from November 4th onwards have created uncertainty and a lack of clarity … For businesses and inward investments to thrive inside the Kingdom, the norms of the rule of law must be observed and transparency maintained … It is also important to remember that most of the merchants of Saudi Arabia have made their wealth through relationships with those in power at one time or another. It would be prudent for MbS to offer a one-off deal — for example on late taxes due on their wealth — to all merchants, without exception or preference."

Instead of a hastily formed "Supreme Committee" tackling corruption, the campaign could be prosecuted with transparency and fair application of the law to all Saudi citizens regardless of family name or "wasta" (privilege, connection).  That would be a radical and dramatic departure from past practice.

Let Saudi Crown Prince Mohammed bin Salman take what he wants from the princes. They add nothing to the national economy. The princes constitute a financial and moral burden on the state. Yet it is critical that he distinguish between the wealth attained by legitimate businessmen and the wealth that pervades the royal family.  The aggressive entry of the royal family in the business sector in the last three decades has led to disastrous effects for the general population and economy. Royals and their agents have received grants of millions of square meters of lands, which raised the cost of the housing for the poor. They obtained licenses to dig deep wells to obtain water for unjustifiable wheat farms, to sell at a subsidized price. They destroyed water reservoirs for upcoming generations. The royal family contributed in creating a corrupt class of businessman who served as nothing more than a front for their greed, tainting the entire business community unfairly.

If Mohammed bin Salman wants to deal properly with corruption, he must preserve two elements vital to the Saudi economy: trust in the state and the role of national companies. If a businessman loses trust in the state, he will not continue investing. Instead, he will take his capital and expertise elsewhere. Second, Mohammed bin Salman must consider the enormous contracting companies and commercial agencies as national treasures. These institutions have gained immense experience and huge international and domestic reputations. They possess institutional memory that is irreplaceable.

New laws must be drafted that both define and prevent corruption from reoccurring, especially laws that will keep Royals away from business, unless they give up their titles, stipend and, more importantly, their government positions. Fighting corruption is complicated, but it is essential that Mohammed bin Salman's actions

be more transparent, for the sake of Saudi Arabia.

# Chapter Eleven:

## A total mess in Lebanon

He said that as if we Arabs need another crisis in our shattered world — but that's exactly what's coming after the mysterious resignation of Lebanese Prime Minister Saad Hariri from Riyadh last Saturday and declarations from the Saudi royal court that Iran has officially crossed a red line.

Now Saudi Arabia has created a problem for itself with some of its staunchest allies: the Sunnis of Lebanon. Even the Sunnis are aligning with different sects, some who are not friendly to Riyadh, to demand the return of Hariri, also a Sunni. It will be impossible to elect a new prime minister in Lebanon unless Hariri is returned. That is a new predicament that Saudi Crown Prince Mohammed bin Salman, also known as MBS, has created — and now needs to solve.

Saudi Arabia has its justification to declare war against Hezbollah: The kingdom, as the young Saudi hawk and minister Thamer al-Sabhan recently declared, no longer distinguishes between the group and the Lebanese government.

The impulsivity of MBS has been a consistent theme — from the war in Yemen to the wave of arrests of constructive critics, royals and senior officials accused of corruption. The severity of Saudi

Arabia's action against Lebanon mirrors the blockade of Qatar in June — abrupt, with no room for negotiation. In the first days of the Saudi campaign against Qatar, supported by Bahrain, Egypt and the United Arab Emirates, the heated rhetoric and actions seemed to indicate that it would be only a matter of time before military intervention in Doha.

Hezbollah, according to Sabhan, has become "a tool of death and destruction" against the kingdom — including training Saudi Shiite terrorists and helping Houthis build Iranian missiles, one of which almost landed at the Riyadh airport this month — and Lebanon will be treated as though it had declared war on Saudi Arabia.

Despite Saudi rhetoric and Lebanese needs, there isn't sufficient political will in Beirut or capacity in Riyadh to take on Hezbollah. No Lebanese fighting force comes close to matching the group's firepower. Saudi Arabia is certainly not going to commit its scarce resources to prosecuting another war while the conflict in Yemen grinds on.

There have been rumors of Israeli-Saudi discussions over attacking Hezbollah, both directly and through President Trump's son-in-law, Jared Kushner. If true, the reports of late-night meetings between MBS and Kushner at the end of October, as well as

Kushner's trip to Israel, take on new meaning considering the events that have followed.

Lebanon finds itself in a bind: It wants to have good tourism and investment relations with Saudi Arabia. At the same time, it sees what Hezbollah is doing in Lebanon and, more important, next door in Syria, where its members fight rebels and support a dictator. Hariri was sincere in his resignation speech when he said Hezbollah was a state within a state — and one that made him fear for his life.

Saudi Arabia has historically attempted to influence politics in Beirut. Saudi Arabia forbade its citizens from traveling to Lebanon in February 2016 and threatened to boycott the Lebanese government unless it cut ties with Hezbollah. Saudi Arabia also endorsed a settlement to elect Michel Aoun as president, who has close ties to Hezbollah, and to elect Hariri as prime minister in an attempt to embrace key Hezbollah allies to win their loyalty and create a rift with a critical ally of Iran.

Hariri's sudden resignation is a clear sign that MBS no longer favors back-channel pressure on Lebanon.

This pivot could in part be due to the "Trump effect," particularly the U.S. president's strong bond with MBS. The two despise Iran and its proxy Hezbollah, a sentiment the Israelis share. Would Trump support the Saudis if they choose to bring Hezbollah down in a war or a Qatari-style blockade? Given the recent rush of the French president — Lebanon's longtime ally — to Riyadh to check in on Hariri, the Saudis will need Trump's help.

Today, Saudi Arabia alone is the most politically stable and economically secure country in the region. Neither the kingdom nor our conflict-ridden region can afford to see my country lose its footing. MBS's rash actions are deepening tensions and undermining the security of the Gulf states and the region as a whole.

# Chapter Twelve:

## Controlling the media

He said that when many of Saudi Arabia's media tycoons ended up in Riyadh's Ritz-Carlton along with more than 300 royals, senior officials and wealthy businessmen accused of corruption, many people assumed that the kingdom's strongman, Crown Prince Mohammed bin Salman, aims to control the media, too. This is far from true, simply because he already does.

Waleed al-Ibrahim, chairman of the Middle East Broadcasting Center (MBC), the most influential TV network throughout the Arab world, was detained along with others last November. He was recently released after making an undisclosed deal with the government. Saudi media reports that while he remains a director in the company, the government's investment fund now controls MBC. Several others caught up in the so-called anti-corruption campaign also held significant media properties among their vast portfolios. Alwaleed bin Talal, now back in his office at Kingdom Holding, owns Rotana entertainment network, a small fraction of his overall $18 billion in wealth. Saleh Kamel owns ART, a network in decline, while his son, who also was arrested and released, is chairman of Okaz newspaper, a popular Saudi daily, and another daily.

It's understandable if one believes this to be a coordinated attack on what is already restricted space for thought and expression in Saudi Arabia, and the wider region. Yet MBS, as the crown prince is known, already controlled the public square long before he arrested family members and senior business elites last November.

MBS and his family already own the Saudi Research & Marketing Group, which includes the pan-Arab daily Al Sharq Al Awsat. Just over a year ago, there was a serious effort to merge with MBC. Differences over the final financial settlement scuttled the talks.

Over the past 18 months, MBS's communications team within the Royal Court publicly has chastised, and worse, intimidated anyone who disagrees. Saud Al-Qahtani, leader of that unit, has a blacklist and calls for Saudis to add names to it. Writers like me, whose criticism is offered respectfully, seem to be considered more dangerous than the more strident Saudi opposition based in London. The government arrested dozens of intellectuals, clerics and social media figures over the past year, even though most are actually supportive of MBS's reforms. Compliant journalists are rewarded with money and access to senior officials.

MBS has full control over the broadcast and digital content that is produced in the kingdom. While it is still possible to access Google, Facebook, Twitter and other sites, the highly orchestrated campaign to align behind him and his 2030 vision has sucked the oxygen from the once-limited but present public square. You can read, of course, but just think twice about sharing or liking whatever isn't fully in line with the official government groupthink.

And if the motive of the crackdown on corruption was to benefit Saudi government coffers, then seizing these business leaders and their assets has backfired. Both Alwaleed and Ibrahim's net worth plummeted while they were held. Those assets seized are worth far less than they were before the crackdown.

Now, as the government's "guests" depart and the Ritz-Carlton prepares for Valentine's Day — the first time that holiday can be openly celebrated in Saudi Arabia — MBS must find a way to revive the value of these important assets and the overall economy. Encouraging public debate and discussion by relaxing his grip on the country's media, as well as releasing those jailed for expressing their views, would prove that he is indeed a true reformer.

# References


- Jamal Khashoggi's columns for The Washington Post, https://www.washingtonpost.com/people/jamalkhashoggi/?utm_term=.1a039f61e3c3

- An Interview with Jamal Khashoggi, Publication: Terrorism Monitor Volume: 2 Issue: 14, By: Mahan Abedin, May 3, 2005 05:35 PM Age: 13 years. https://jamestown.org/interview/an-interview-with-jamal-khashoggi/

- Wikipedia, Jamal Ahmad Khashoggi, https://en.wikipedia.org/wiki/Jamal_Khashoggi